APPALACHIA
. . . A Special Place
. . . A Bridge of Hope

by

Reverend Ralph Beiting
Founder of the Christian Appalachian Project

(Cover photo by Ellen Burke)

This book was written to commemorate the
25th Anniversary of the
Christian Appalachian Project.
It is dedicated to the thousands of
poor people CAP has been fortunate enough
to serve over the years.

The Christian Appalachian Project
1965–1990

PROLOGUE

For forty years Reverend Ralph W. Beiting has worked to ease the pain caused by the terrible poverty that afflicts the people who live in the Appalachian mountains of Eastern Kentucky. More than twenty five years ago he founded the Christian Appalachian Project (CAP). CAP is an interdenominational Christian organization that provides emergency relief, help with housing, educational programs, business development programs and visitation programs for the elderly. Through the generous work of thousands of volunteers CAP has become one of the largest relief organizations working to help Americans.

Reverend Beiting suffered a serious automobile accident in January, 1990. He wrote this book while recovering from his injuries.

TABLE OF CONTENTS

Prologue

Building Bridges

A few days ago I almost lost my life. I fell asleep at the wheel of the van I was driving and crashed into the rear of a coal truck.

At first I didn't feel anything, but I was terrified of the horrible noise, the worst noise I've ever heard. It was the sound of shattering glass and crumpling metal and screeching tires. Somewhere mixed in was the sound of my own bones breaking.

It could very well have been the last noise I ever heard.

I was driving to visit two struggling companies and see if there was anything I could do to help them stay in business and continue to employ people in this area of extremely high unemployment.

As I drove I began to feel drowsy and I should have stopped for a rest. But I had a schedule to keep and my hours are packed so tightly these days that I rarely have time to rest.

I opened a can of soft drink and tried to wake up, but I grew more and more weary with each mile. The last thing I remember thinking was that I should shut off the speed control on the van and

try to wake up. After driving more than two
million miles of Kentucky roads in the 40 years
since I started working to help the poor in Appalachia, it didn't occur to me that I could be in real
danger.

Then I heard that horrible noise.

It screamed in my ears and woke me instantly. I
saw glass everywhere. The inside of the van was a
disaster. The doors were crushed. I felt terrible
pains in my leg and chest, and for the first few
moments I thought I had reached the end . . . that
I was going to die.

In that moment my thoughts turned to our Lord
Jesus. All I could do was repeat His name, "Jesus,
Jesus, I love You." I told Him I was sorry for all
my sins and shortcomings. I called on our holy
Mother Mary, and asked for her help. I prayed
that I could be with them if this were my time to
die.

After a few moments I began to sense that I was
not dying. I was in great pain and in great trouble,
but I was going to have to live and endure and
continue my work. My thoughts turned then to
survival. I knew I had to get out of that twisted
van—and quickly.

I struggled to no avail. My right knee was
pinned securely under the dashboard. The more I
struggled the more it hurt, but it didn't come free.
My other leg was free. My right arm was cut and
bleeding, and my left arm was so sore I could barely

move it. Never in my life had I felt so helpless. I am a big man, six foot tall and 260 pounds. I have always been strong enough to do whatever I put my mind to do physically. But now I was at the mercy of a trap of steel. I was terrified.

After what seemed like an eternity, but was in reality just a few minutes, a state police trooper approached the window of the van. The young man tried very hard to relax me, God bless him, but all he could say was, "Don't worry. We'll have you out in a few minutes. Don't be afraid. Don't worry about the smoke. It's just anti-freeze."

I told him I wasn't going anywhere and that I'd wait as patiently as I could. He was a very young man. I hope someday I can thank him for his help and his concern for my life.

Before long a crowd of people gathered around the van, and I heard them excitedly discussing how to get me out. Unfortunately, I heard the voices agreeing that there was no way to open the door. As they tried to figure out how to get me out of my terrible trap, I noticed a different kind of smoke coming from under what was left of the dash. It was gray smoke and didn't smell like anti-freeze. I motioned to the police officer and told him that I thought something was on fire and that my leg felt hot. He ran to his cruiser and returned with a fire extinguisher. He sprayed it under the van and under the coal truck where my van was wedged. The fumes from the extinguisher were worse than the smoke, and I could hardly breathe. Finally, the extinguisher ran out, but the smoke still billowed and I heard people say the van was on fire. Once again I began to think that my time had come. Terrified, I remembered that I had just filled up with gas and was carrying 40 gallons—more than enough to explode the van into charred ashes.

When I began my work in Appalachia 40 years ago I was caught in a cistern explosion and my hair and clothing caught on fire. My mind went back to that memory and the pain and terror. I asked God to use my suffering—if this were the way I were to die—to bless the people for whom I started the Christian Appalachian Project—the poor and lonely people of Appalachia. I prayed for all our supporters. I hoped that my final act could be an act of love for the people of the mountains, the old, the young, the mothers and fathers—all those children of God who suffer so much every day of their lives.

As I sat waiting to be consumed by fire I asked Him to bless His church, because through the church Christ reaches out to all people. Then I prepared myself for the pain. I prayed for courage.

But this was not my time to go.

After a few minutes, a little fire truck from a tiny community called Feisty pulled up. Feisty is so small that it doesn't appear on any map of Kentucky, but a dozen years ago I preached Christ in its streets. Perhaps this was His way of saying thank you. In any event, the good people of Feisty will now always hold a special place in my heart. The firefighters unrolled their hoses and got right to work. They drenched the van and the coal truck and I felt water running down my legs. Soon the smoke cleared and I began to feel safe again.

A few hours later I was out of the van and on my way to a hospital. There they patched me up as well as possible and a week later packed me off to a convalescent home to recuperate and continue rehabilitation therapy.

That's where I am today. And I must admit that for the briefest moment I wondered why God would allow me to come to this fate. I thought about all the work that now wouldn't get done and I wondered why this happened.

As I lie here with a broken leg, lacerations on one arm and a cast on the other, a broken jaw and a broken nose, I keep thinking about my hands, the parts of my body that are least injured.

I look at my hands, and I think back to my boyhood. I remember how my hands were my strength. As the oldest in a family of eleven children growing up in the Depression, I had a great deal of responsibility and my hands were invaluable. I used them to feed chickens and milk cows. I used them to wield a shovel to turn the soil in our garden, to swing a scythe to cut hay for the cows, and to wield a pitchfork to stack the hay in the barn.

I learned to use my hands for gentle things, like the handshake of friendship, a touch of compassion or a helping hand to those—old and young—whose steps were not steady. I used my hands to turn the pages of a book when I was learning to read. Later I used them to turn the pages of the Bible when I learned to pray. As a priest I learned to use my hands to bring the body and blood of Christ to those who hungered for His communion.

I also learned to build. My father was a carpenter, so I learned to use a hammer and saw. I learned to build homes, and furniture, and tools . . . but most of all I learned to build bridges.

I have always been fascinated by bridges. To me they represent the greatest impulses of our humanity and our technology. Unlike weapons that destroy and tear people apart, unlike even houses and buildings that can sometimes isolate and imprison people, bridges exist for only one reason—to bring people together who could not otherwise touch.

I'm speaking not only of physical bridges that bring people together across rivers and gorges, but also of emotional and spiritual bridges that bring people together across the gaps of wealth and poverty, race, creed and generation.

Since my youth I've wanted to build those bridges with my own hands. Forty years ago I was given a great chance. I was presented with the challenge to build bridges between the affluent and God's special people of Appalachia. I was challenged to build bridges between the people of Appalachia themselves, who are often isolated behind and between steep mountain gorges and hollows. I was challenged to build bridges between 20th century America and a mountain people who often live in conditions more like the 19th or even 18th centuries. I was challenged to build bridges of common faith between different denominations of God's children.

That's why I started the Christian Appalachian Project. I wanted to help Christian people all over the country reach out to their brothers and sisters in Appalachia. Though I am a Catholic priest, I called it the Christian Appalachian Project rather than the Catholic Appalachian Project because I wanted it to be an inclusive organization, not an exclusive one. I called it a project because I wanted it to be an organization of work.

It takes work to build bridges, not talk or theorizing. Over the years CAP, as we call the Christian Appalachian Project, has done a great deal of work to repair people's houses, to bring them food and clothing, and to help them get medical care. We have worked to teach people to read, to write, and to master the ways of the 20th century American economy. We have put in millions of hours of sweat and blood.

I pray that in those hours I have been at least a

little successful in building bridges, and I hope that the work of building those bridges will continue long after my death. I believe that in some ways this accident was to remind me of my mortality and make me realize that the job of building bridges is not over . . . that there is still a great deal to accomplish and little time left.

I think our Lord wanted me to have time to re-arrange my thoughts and gain a new perspective for a final push in my life. In these last few days I've had more time for simple contemplation than at any time since I came to Appalachia. I know that in the next few months, as I recover, I'll have a lot more time to think and plan and prepare for the time I have left to give.

I want to use this time to put down my thoughts on building bridges in Appalachia so that no matter what happens to me, the work will continue—it is far too important to be left without direction.

Many people simply throw up their hands when they first come to Appalachia and are confronted with the problems we face—abject poverty, high illiteracy rates, generations of alcohol abuse and physical abuse. All they see are the problems.

When I look at Appalachia I see potential. I see resourceful, hard-working people who live isolated from all the creature comforts most of us consider necessary to modern life. I see strong families. I see a strong, simple faith in God. I see intelligence waiting to blossom under the guidance of education.

Of course, I also see the poverty. I see a great need to heal. Sometimes when I drive through these magnificent mountains, one of God's greatest creations, I want to cry. I see creeks that once bubbled forth with good water, now polluted and cluttered with trash. I see little valleys covered, not only with God's beautiful trees, but also with rusted automobiles and burned shells of abandoned houses.

I'm not blind. I see the physical poverty everyone else sees. But to me that is only part of the true picture. The true poverty in Appalachia is a poverty of the spirit.

The true poverty is represented by children who no longer dream about the future. It is found in parents who want the good things all parents want for their children—and who have to settle for whatever they can get. It is glaringly obvious in young people who start their adult lives without even the prospect of a job. It is heart-rendingly obvious in old people who reach the golden years of their lives and find themselves outcasts, living in poverty and isolation and uselessness.

I see this poverty of the human spirit even more clearly than others see the physical signs of poverty in Appalachia.

But in that poverty of the spirit, I also see signs of hope. We don't need billions of dollars to revamp the roads and schools and facilities of Appalachia. If we can give people hope, if we can end the poverty of the spirit by building bridges of love and friendship, the Appalachian people will rise up and become real partners in the struggle to end the physical poverty they face.

I see the poverty everyone else sees. But I see the potential even more clearly. I know we can build bridges between God and His people—bridges between the affluent and the poor, between the old and the young, between mainstream America and Appalachia.

The amazing thing is that if we Americans build these bridges, we will become truly free. People who ignore the least of their brothers and sisters can never be truly free. I believe that when you solve one problem you solve many problems. By helping build bridges in Appalachia, we free ourselves from selfishness and greed and all the other vices that keep us from putting God and His people at the center of our world.

Today I cannot see the blue-green mountains I love so much. I lie here in my small room staring at white walls, alone with my thoughts. But I know the mountains are still there. I know the people are still there. I know the pain in their hearts is still there and I know their dreams are still alive. I hope by writing this book I can stir others to know of that pain and help me make those dreams reality in the coming months and years. I can delude myself no longer—and maybe that was God's purpose—I cannot do this job alone. I may never have the mobility I had at the start of 1990.

I openly ask each of you who reads this book and feels the pain of the Appalachian people to help me in whatever way you can. Come and volunteer, send money to support our work, bring industry and jobs to Appalachia, donate food, clothing, books—whatever you can do will help.

Above all, pray for us.

The motto of our beautiful state of Kentucky is "United we stand, divided we fall." It has always been my dream that we might be able to live that motto and build bridges that once again unite the people of Appalachia with the rest of America.

Lying here in a convalescent home, unable to move without assistance, I think about how interdependent we all are. It seems to me that America and the world at large have become very isolated. We have mass communication and instant news sources. Highways stretch across the nation, joining every state and every town. Hop on a jet and you can fly from New York to Los Angeles in less than five hours. But somehow all this has not brought us happiness. It has not brought us closer together.

With all our technology and wealth, we haven't taken the time to build enough bridges.

In the following pages I hope I can describe some of the bridges CAP has built with the help of the people of Appalachia and thousands of volunteers and supporters who care about the people of

Appalachia. I hope I can show how those bridges have helped people, and that there are many bridges left to build, before we can be one family of God.

Please pray for my recovery from this accident, and most of all, pray for God's special children of Appalachia.

Between God's People

I was once nearly arrested for preaching about Jesus. I remember the day as clearly as if it were yesterday. I set out with several seminarians and others to preach and sing in the streets and reach out to the people of Martin County, Kentucky. This is in the area infamous for the Hatfields and McCoys and generations of violence.

I was preaching in Inez, the county seat, and as I told the people of God's love, a sheriff's car pulled up. The driver rushed up to me, began cussing, and told me in no uncertain terms that I had to stop preaching. I had already obtained permission from the mayor and the city police chief to preach in that particular spot, but I could not convince the man. He kept yelling and swearing that he was going to arrest me if we didn't pack up in five minutes and move on. He pulled his gun and said he'd take me to the jail and lock me up.

He got my temper up, I'm sorry to say, and I began to argue with him. He seemed deaf to my persuasions, so finally I told the crowd that we would be moving on, outside the town. The man stood threateningly, with his gun drawn, while we dismantled and packed our equipment.

Before we drove away, another man came up and asked me why we were stopping. He said he really enjoyed our preaching and wanted to hear more. I told him we had to stop because of the deputy sheriff with the gun. He tried to talk to the irate deputy but had no more luck than I had. He told me he was astonished at the man's ignorance. He said that what I was preaching—God's love for us all—was exactly what the people needed to hear. Then he reached into his pocket and gave me a five dollar bill.

He said, "I hope you won't think we're all like that man and that you'll continue to preach."

I often think about that gentleman. I think when he offered us that five dollars, it was more than just a donation. It was a plea—it was a prayer that bridges be built, that ideas be communicated, and that God's people learn to love each other.

It is for people like this man that I have been street preaching for more than 40 years in Appalachia. I may be the only Catholic priest in America who preaches in the streets regularly, but I believe we must fulfill Jesus' command to, "Go into all the world and preach the gospel to all creation."

Every summer I gather a group of other priests, nuns, lay people, seminarians, and protestant ministers—anyone I can con. For several weeks we move from one town to another. In each town we pick a spot—in front of the general store, or the town hall, or even in someone's front yard. We set up a few amplifiers and put on a program of Bible readings, preaching, praying and singing.

By doing this we bring the Good News of Christ to the people, many of whom are unchurched. We meet people one-on-one and learn about their problems and challenges in a way that we could not otherwise.

And we build long-lasting bridges between God's people.

Although I was raised a Catholic and love the Catholic faith so much that I have dedicated my life to it as a Catholic priest, I know Baptists and Lutherans worship the same Risen Lord and the same God. I know that Jesus said, "Whoever is not against us is with us." And I know that only when all of God's people join together can we end the poverty and despair of His people.

I have always looked for ways that I can meet other people of God halfway and even go that extra step. But people who have been isolated as long as the people of Appalachia are usually mistrustful of outsiders. When I first came to Eastern Kentucky there were five Catholics in the county where I started my first church. In all of Eastern Kentucky there weren't more than five thousand Catholics. Generations of mistrust had instilled in the people a fear of Catholics, and as a priest I was the embodiment of that fear. Most people had never even met a Catholic, yet they were convinced we were evil and murderous and blasphemous.

I don't fault the Appalachian people for these prejudices. These fears came to America from Medieval Europe and thrived in the isolation of Appalachia. Through the centuries, Catholics have been guilty of the same kind of prejudices towards protestants and other believers. That's why we need to build bridges between all of God's people.

I remember another occasion when I was street preaching some years ago. At that time we didn't have the battery-operated amplifiers we have now, and I needed to run an extension cord to plug in our equipment. I saw a man sitting on his porch so I asked if it would be possible to use his electricity to put on our program. He asked me what kind of program it was, and I said it would be a religious program about Jesus. He said he liked Jesus, so it would be all right with him.

I went back to the car and returned dragging an extension cord. As I was about to plug it into a receptacle on the porch he said, "Brother, I didn't ask you, what kind of religion are you?"

I told him I was a Catholic priest.

His face immediately hardened, and he told me that I could forget about plugging in the cord. He didn't "hold" with Catholics and there was no way he was going to let me preach in front of his house.

The spot in front of his yard was the best spot in the area and he had aroused my curiosity, so I wasn't about to give up that easily. I asked him, "What if I came to you and asked you in Jesus' name for a cup of water? Would you give me a cup of water, even though I'm a Catholic priest?"

This troubled him. He told me that it says in the Bible he had to give me a cup of water if I asked in Jesus' name.

"Well," I said, "What I'm asking you for isn't very different. All I'm asking for is a plug full of electricity."

Now the old man was truly troubled. He told me he was a Baptist preacher, and that he didn't know what I was trying to do to him, but he was afraid to do anything that might hurt Jesus, so he agreed to let me use the electricity. He told me that if I said anything he didn't like he would pull the plug.

That was fair enough, so I set up and we read the Bible and preached and sang, and told the people about God's love.

After we were done he asked me if I could forgive him. I told him he did me a favor and I had nothing to forgive him for, but he insisted.

He said, "I almost didn't let you preach here. Everything you said about Jesus was good. It made me proud to believe in Him. You made the people of this community feel good about God and themselves. You made them happier."

He made me promise that if I came back to his town I would plug my equipment in on his porch again. Three years in a row we went back there, and he and I became good friends. Then a few years went by before I could get back that way again, and when I did, his wife told me he had passed away the winter before.

She told me that on the day he died he told her, "If that Catholic preacher ever comes back again, be sure to let him have electricity and let him know I want him to talk about Jesus."

I think about him a lot. He was different from me. He was a mountain man and I had grown up outside the mountains. He was a Baptist and I was a Roman Catholic. The only things we had in common were a love of Jesus and a love of the mountains. But because of Jesus and His Word, we became friends and partners in the mountains we both loved.

Together he and I built a beautiful bridge that day, between his church and mine, between his heart and mine, between his understanding of God and mine.

The other day I was lying in my bed recovering, and one of the local priests, Father Rock, came in to bring me Communion. As we talked, a gentleman in a hospital gown came into the room, leaning on his cane as he walked. He watched while I received Communion, and then he came a little closer to the bed. Father Rock asked him if there were something he could do for him. The man said that he had heard on the radio that I was badly hurt and in the same hospital where he was. He wanted to see me because he was very grateful to me.

He then told the story of how I had come to his town in Breathitt County in the early '60s. I lived there in a trailer, along the Kentucky River. I started a Bible school there and met this man at the hardware store he ran in town. I don't think I had seen him in the more than 20 years since. He told me how much he appreciated what I did for Breathitt County and for all the mountain people, and that he was proud to know me, even though he was certainly not a Catholic. His simple gratitude and his image of the bridge we had built between us brought tears to my eyes. It made me feel wonderful to think that he remembered after all these years.

I remember that we bought a piece of land in his town to build a church. The Corps of Army Engineers had taken a huge horseshoe bend of the Kentucky River and changed the course of the river so they could build a highway. There was some farmland right on the roadway that I thought was a wonderful place for a house of God. I asked around to find out who owned the land, but people told me that the man would never sell it. He had already refused a bank, a motel, and a restaurant. The people told me that as an outsider—

and someone who wanted to build a Catholic church—I didn't stand a chance.

But I know there is no such thing as chance, so I decided to work harder than ever to get that lovely piece of property. I found out where the man worked. He was a part-time carpenter and was working on a house that morning. I found him where he was working and approached him. He recognized me by my clothes—I was the only priest in nearly a hundred miles—and told me he had heard I was looking for him. He asked if I were one of "those Catholic fellows." I told him I was. He said he needed a break, so he'd take me over to see his land.

We jumped in his pickup truck and drove over to the property. He spent the next hour walking me all over, showing me one lovely spot after another. Finally he asked me what I thought. I told him it was beautiful property and that he ought to be proud to own it.

He looked at me rather puzzled and said, "You sure don't know much about buying land, do you?"

I asked him what he meant by that, and he said I should tell him all the things that were wrong with the land and why he should be happy to get rid of it at a pretty cheap price.

I felt that if I told him what I truly believed we could become friends, whether or not I bought his property. "I wouldn't want to lie to you," I said.

He looked at me even more strangely, and thought a minute. "You know, there's only one thing God ain't making no more of, and that's land. I appreciate a man who loves land and who can tell the truth about it. How much land do you need for the church?"

When I recovered from my shock, I outlined an area between an acre and a half and two acres. He told me he would sell the land at a price that was very reasonable. A year later we built a lovely little church on that piece of land.

Another year or so went by before he sold or rented any more of his land. Eventually a motel went up, and a school, and a restaurant, and some much needed new homes. I can't help but think that if I hadn't built a bridge with that man by telling him his land was beautiful, the church and all those other facilities and businesses the community urgently needed would not have been built.

As I was being wheeled out of my room on a stretcher down to the nurse's station the other day, a woman came up and asked me if I remembered her. I admitted that I didn't. She said, "Do you remember Lost Creek and a ball game?"

When she said that, a wonderful day 25 years ago came rushing back to me. Lost Creek is well-named because you have to get off the main roads and onto secondary roads and then off those roads onto dirt roads before you finally come to Lost Creek. During one of my street preaching journeys, I had taken a group of about eight seminarians back into that area. It was so isolated and sparsely populated that there wasn't really any place to preach. I usually try to find a spot where at least a dozen families live. But for some reason I felt in my heart that we needed to be in Lost Creek that day.

It was late afternoon and we probably should have given up and gone back to our trailer to fix dinner and get ready for an evening of preaching somewhere else. But sometimes I do foolish things, so we went further into Lost Creek. We came to this little house, perched on the other side of the creek, across a swinging bridge. There we met a woman who had six or seven little children running barefoot around her. I told her we were visiting the area, that we were preaching about God, and that we'd probably be preaching that night in Jackson.

She said she hadn't been in church for years because there was no church around that she belonged to. She said she was truly lonely and had a yearning in her heart for the Word of God. She said she was concerned about her children who were not learning about God as she wanted them to. The woman's need was so moving that I suggested to the seminarians that we unpack the sandwiches we had with us and eat there.

After supper, instead of preaching, we played baseball with her children and three or four of the other kids who lived in the area. After it grew too dark to see the ball anymore, we sat on the porch and talked about God with the family. It was a wonderful break from our preaching and it felt good to reach out to a lonely woman and those wonderful children.

I didn't see the woman after that, but when we got land and built a church in Jackson she heard about it and attended every Sunday.

She made the trip of about forty miles to visit me in the hospital and tell me how much she appreciated that day when we stopped to play baseball with her kids. Her children are all grown now, with children of their own, but she said none of them has ever forgotten the day the Catholic priest and the seminarians stopped the world to play baseball with them.

It's amazing to me the bridges we can build without even knowing it. I had no specific plan when we decided to stay with that family. It just seemed like a friendly thing to do and seemed as if we were filling a need for this isolated family of God's children.

Another day when I was still in a lot of pain and not really hoping for visitors at the hospital, a man came in to see me. I immediately recognized him by his unusual mustache. He was from Knott County, a town called Topmost.

I met him a few years ago when we received a donation of chairs and desks from an AT&T office in New Jersey. There were far more desks and chairs than we could use, so we stored the furniture in our warehouse in Prestonsburg. I was trying to figure out how to distribute the furniture to other organizations that needed it, when this man came in and asked how much I wanted for a few desks and chairs. I told him they were not for sale and asked him what he would do with them if he had them.

He told me he was the pastor of the Topmost Baptist Church and needed the desks for a classroom, and chairs for the church sanctuary. I told him he could have whatever he needed. He looked me in the eye and said, "I thought you were a Catholic priest."

"Well yes, I am," I replied.

"Didn't you hear me say I was a Baptist preacher?"

"Yes I heard that," I said.

"Doesn't that make a difference whether you give them to me for nothing or charge me for them?" he asked.

I said that if he were going to use them for God's work, that was enough for me. He was still shaking his head in disbelief when he left with some desks and about thirty chairs.

The following Christmas when we wanted to put on a Christmas service in his county, that man generously offered his church to us. When the time came for me to preach, he stood up and told the congregation the whole story of the chairs and desks. Then he said that he was going to take the money the church had set aside to buy furniture, and use it to buy food for the needy.

The church had never given anything to the needy because its members were themselves so needy. But he felt that because the Christian Appalachian Project had given something to them, they should give something to someone even needier than themselves. It was a wonderful gesture that showed the true spirit of Christ and Christmas, and it came about because he and I had built a bridge between our two churches.

When he came to see me at the hospital, he told me I had to be more careful. He said, "We can't afford to have you die. What will all the rest of us do if we don't have you here to help us and support us, so that we can care for God and His people?"

I could hardly believe my ears. How things have changed from the days when I was routinely run off for preaching, when people threatened me with guns and tried to arrest me.

He told me that this past Christmas, his congregation managed to raise enough money to help twice as many people as it had that first year. Somehow, in building a bridge between our church and that pastor, we have helped build a bridge between that Baptist congregation and its own needy.

These stories remind me of how much things have changed. Bridges made of steel and stone decay and crumble, but the bridges of love and friendship we have built between God's people here in Appalachia grow stronger and stronger with each passing year. Old hatreds are disappearing, and fears are being replaced with trust and love. Today most of my friends are not Catholic— something I would never have predicted 40 years ago. Many of those who care for me most deeply are the people who have other churches or who have no church at all.

Hand-in-hand we are walking toward our heavenly Father across the bridges we have built together.

Between the 19th Century and the 20th

The 20th century has been a miraculous time. We have conquered the atom, brought electricity and telephones to every town, and even traveled to the moon. Yet for many people in America, the 20th century has not yet arrived.

I have met far too many families like Janet's. Janet lived with her husband and four children in an abandoned bus. They cut a hole in the roof for a smokestack for their wood stove. They had no electricity, so they dug a hole in the ground to try and keep food cold. They used an outhouse for a bathroom.

They were living a 19th century life in the midst of our land of plenty.

Janet told me of her great sadness that her children had to live this way, when all around them they saw great wealth and comfort. She was saddened and angered that their lives seemed to mean so little.

I asked her how we could help. She told me that a neighbor had agreed to let her rent some land to grow crops. Janet needed $2,500 to buy seeds and fertilizer and have the land plowed. She would pay

the rent after she harvested her crop. She had such
great determination that I was sure she would succeed against all odds, so CAP loaned her the
$2,500.

The first year Janet farmed she had a very good
crop and the second year she did even better. She
did so well that she was able to keep up her pay-
ments on the $2,500 and still find a better place for
her family to live.

Our simple act of faith in lending her $2,500 was
the bridge that allowed her and her family to cross
from the 19th to the 20th century. They have a
long way to go before they complete the journey,
but now the bridge is there for them.

One of CAP's most important missions is building that bridge between the 19th century and the
20th. In the 19th century life was harder than today, but everyone endured together and people at
least had the self-respect and pride that comes
from being in the mainstream of society.

Today, people who live in poverty are bombard-
ed by the flagrant wealth of others. They see the
flashy cars, and the fine food and creature comforts that fill fancy homes, and the despair be-
comes even more painful than the poverty.

One of Appalachia's most desperate needs is
good housing. Too many families live in run-down
trailers or buses or even cars. The houses people
have are often falling apart. They don't have insu-
lation or indoor plumbing. Many are heated with

makeshift wood or coal stoves. This, combined with ancient or faulty wiring, makes fires almost inevitable. Once a fire starts, the house usually burns to the ground before fire trucks can reach the isolated hollows where the people live.

One of CAP's most important programs is our Home Repair Program. We identify those families that have the greatest need and help them improve their houses by supplying materials and volunteer labor. The people pay us back for the materials in small installments. This way we stretch our funding—and the families develop pride in their homes.

I know a family struggling to raise three young boys. Their job is even harder than usual because one of the boys has Perthes Disease. The disease causes severe pain in his hips and makes him walk with a limp. Doctors told his parents that one of the best treatments to relieve the pain is a hot bath twice a day.

Unfortunately they didn't have a bathroom.

The boy's father is a disabled coal miner, and they couldn't afford to install a bathroom or a hot water heater. CAP provided the materials, and the boy's father and uncle built a bathroom onto their little house. We also provided a hot water heater and fuel. Now the little boy can take hot baths, and he is feeling much better.

He's a plucky kid. Despite his Perthes Disease he is active and bright. He even plays on the local little league team and I'm told he is quite a hitter.

Again, just a little wood and some plumbing supplies created a bridge to the 20th century that greatly improved the life of a family.

The people of the mountains are independent folk. They don't want handouts and they resent paternalistic charity. But they do need a helping hand and they treasure honest friendship.

Last summer a man tried several times to reach me. He repeatedly left messages saying that he desperately needed a job and he would do anything for work. At first I was not very open to his pleas. I told someone to call him back and tell him we couldn't pay our own bills right now so we couldn't help him. Then I said to myself, "Oh for goodness sakes, at least talk to the man."

I found out he had recently been laid off from his job. He and his family had been renting a trailer but they were unable to pay the rent and had been put out. Now they were living in their car, surviving day to day.

I told him we were in bad shape ourselves but that I would take a walk of faith with him. I said, "I'll give you a job working here at the church, and I'll hope and pray that by the end of the week I'll find some way to pay you."

I asked him how much he needed to get by.

He said, "I'll work for a dollar an hour. If I work ten hours a day, six days a week, that will give me $60 a week. That's $60 more than I have now."

I told him I would pay him $4.50 an hour, but that I didn't know how long it would last. He worked for me throughout the summer and he turned out to be such a wonderful person and such a hard worker that as summer came to an end, I drew him aside and said, "I don't know how I can do it, but I know you need a regular job. I'll pay you $12,000 a year. You are free to get another job if you find something better."

With that he was able to rent a trailer and get back on his feet. I kept telling the people at CAP what a dedicated worker he was, so when we needed a new manager for one of our children's camps, we offered him the job, which included health benefits and good housing.

He came to me and said, "The people at CAP have been awfully good to me, and the job seems wonderful, but I'm not going to take it."

I said, "What's the matter with you? Why not?"

"I don't want to give up working for you," he said. "You need so much help and you've been so good to me. I want to stay and repay you."

I told him his family came first and I finally convinced him to take the job.

The day after my accident, he and his wife were the first people to visit me. He said he was so worried about me he couldn't work. He drove 140 miles round-trip just to make sure I was okay and to see if there were anything I needed.

I think back to the day when I learned that he and his family were living in a car, and I thank God that today he has a good job, a secure future and good housing for his loved ones.

They have repaid our generosity many times over. His wife now volunteers in our Attic stores where we provide good quality used clothing at very low prices. She sorts donated clothes and staffs the counter whenever she can. Even the children help out in the stores and wherever else they are needed.

I found that in providing a bridge back to the 20th century for this family I have made some wonderful new friends. Where once there were strangers, there is now a great bond. We have crossed a wide valley and found love and generosity on both sides.

Between the Old and the Young

When I first came to Appalachia in 1946, I was 22 years old. In the enthusiasm of youth, I fell in love with a place I had never known before, and quite frankly, never much cared about. A few years later I returned permanently as an ordained priest and set to work, again with the spirit of youth and recklessness.

Today I am a senior citizen and I find that while I have lost some of the fire of youth, I have a quiet determination and an inner peace that I never had as a young man.

I think that's why I understand the need to build bridges between the old and the young in Appalachia. I know how much we are losing when those people—the young on one shore and the old on the other—remain distant. I have lived through the changes myself, and I understand the people on both shores.

Older people have a great deal to offer to our youth. They have lived through so much and seen so many changes. Many of the old people in Appalachia were young before automobiles were commonplace and before TVs were invented.

They struggled to feed families before there were supermarkets in every town. They farmed and worked hard and lived a full life.

They learned to cope and adapt, and they forged the future that is now the present. They have the wisdom that comes only with living.

We need to regain many of their values and ways of life. Every day we realize more and more that not everything modern is good, and that we are throwing away priceless parts of the heritage that makes this nation unique. Where else can we turn to relearn the things we have lost, but to our elders?

Last year some of our volunteers had an excellent idea to preserve a vital part of that heritage. They formed a quilting club with 20 older women. Quilting has always been a vital part of life in Appalachia. It is a way to record lives and loved ones. It's a way of expressing the joy of life and the love of God. It is a wonderfully social activity that strengthens ties between neighbors and friends.

Yet quilting is dying out today, because the young don't want to learn it. It's too slow a process for today's youth, and it seems to have little practical value when you can buy a machine-made quilt from Korea for $20. The old women who learned quilting at their mothers' knees have lost faith in it and are not passing it on to the young.

That's why I was so pleased to hear that some of our young volunteers had formed this group.

They met on Wednesday nights for coffee. They quilted, conversed and had a wonderful time. The older women shared their lives, and the young people infused their older friends with their spark and enthusiasm.

Last May they presented the completed quilt as a gift to CAP. It now hangs in a place of honor at our building in Lancaster, Kentucky.

It is by far the most beautiful quilt I have ever seen, not only for the wonderful needlework but also for the love that it radiates.

One of the women who worked on the quilt passed away before it was completed. We'll miss her, but I can't help feeling that part of her is still here in that quilt and part of her lives on in the hearts and minds of the young people she taught to quilt.

At the beginning of the project, many of the older women felt the young didn't care about them anymore. Our volunteers built a wonderful bridge between the old and the young with that project, and I'm very proud of them.

Many of them have become quite good quilters, and a wonderful tradition will now survive with at least a few young people.

Many of the elderly I know are terrified. They live in fear that they will not be able to take care of themselves and that no one will ever visit them. They fear they'll have to go to a nursing home, or worst of all, that they will become a burden to their families. This is true not just in Appalachia, of course, but it is especially hard on the elderly here because they have so little money and are so terribly isolated.

I have a friend named Leonard who has led a long and worthwhile life. Drive down the roads near his home, and he'll tell you which ones he built. He still remembers where they had to dynamite and how they had to fill in with stone here, and build a retaining wall there. He worked for many years as a blacksmith with his father. He is one of the original "Mr. Fix-its"—there is no machine he can't have running like a top in minutes.

Leonard's wife died a few years back, and his children long ago moved away. Until recently, he sat in his porch swing every day with his old dog, Tiny, at his feet.

If you visited him he would proudly show you the three most important features of his home: a wood stove he made out of an old oil drum; an old rocking chair that has been in his family for generations; and an old, dusty organ his wife used to play. His eyes well with tears when he recalls his wife, and he keeps all her clothes and things stored safely away.

For years we have visited Leonard, bringing him wood for his stove and helping him get to doctor's appointments. Mostly we have been there to lend an ear and a kind word to a lonely old man.

A few months ago Leonard's infirmities caught up with him. Years ago he suffered from tuberculosis. He now has shingles and he doesn't eat very well anymore. He may also have Alzheimer's Disease. It's impossible for him to live alone any longer, and he has now moved in with relatives.

It saddens me to see Leonard lose his independence and the home he loves so much, but I am proud of the fact that CAP provided the bridge that allowed our volunteers to help Leonard live several more years on his own. We helped him keep his dignity and hold on to the things that were dear to him.

The old don't need sympathy, they need respect. I greatly respect Leonard for the life he built with his own two hands. I wouldn't take that away from him for all the gold in the world. That's why it was so important for CAP to share with him without taking over his life.

We are building wonderful bridges between the senior citizens of Appalachia and our young volunteers. But we also need to rebuild the natural bridges that should exist between Appalachia's old people and her young people. Those bridges have been broken because many of the young move away to find work. They have been broken because children are lured by the false promises of a materialistic and drug-infested society. They have been broken because the young have so little appreciation for the simple faith of their elders. And they have been broken because old people don't see the valuable contributions young people can and do make to society.

One day when I was preaching in a little hollow, fifteen or so youths came up to heckle us. They got louder and louder but we continued the program, preaching and singing. Eventually they quieted down and began to listen. When the program was over, they came over and asked me why I didn't get mad at them. I said I didn't know I was supposed to get mad at them. I had come to be their friend.

They said they were trying to make me angry and couldn't understand why I wasn't.

They told me that earlier that day they had been setting off firecrackers and making noise near an old lady's house, and she had called the police and had them run off her property. The kids said they hated adults.

I tried to listen and hear what they were really saying, and I think they were expressing the loneliness that children suffer when they are cut off from the adult world. I told them I felt sorry for the woman, not because of the noise they had made, but because she missed an opportunity to reach out to them and become their friend. Many times we think that the entire problem rests with the young, but we adults need to take the first steps toward the bridge if we want the young to follow. We have to lead—and not just curse the insolence and disrespect of youth.

The young are looking for guidance. They want discipline. They want advice about how to live and what to value. They need someone to inspire them to greatness.

Too often today our senior citizens are simply retired. I dislike the classic image of the retired old couple: sitting in front of the TV, vacationing in Florida, hiding in their safe house . . . biding time until they pass on.

To me, those of us lucky enough to live to old age are given a great opportunity to live a new life. God did not design us to be a rock or a log. We were meant to be involved. It is the only way to find peace.

Few things are more stressful than the boredom that comes with inaction.

I dream of senior citizens coming from all over the country to live here with us in Appalachia. Imagine what a wonderful retirement life this could be. They could live here in these beautiful mountains and do God's work—work that will make each day precious.

Senior citizens have great assets and talents that would be invaluable to us. We always need more teachers. In most of our counties, more than one third of adults can't read the food labels at the grocery store. Because they are adults they have a hard time humbling themselves to learn to read at the hands of a 22 year old volunteer. Think how much more comfortable they would be learning from an older person.

We need new business ideas and business expertise to help those who want to start businesses in Appalachia. We need adults who can provide day care. We need senior citizens who can befriend the lonely, isolated older people of the mountains.

There are so many ways that we need to shore up the bridge between the old and the young here in Appalachia. There is much to be gained by joining the wisdom and experience of age and the energy and enthusiasm of youth.

A bridge between the old and the young will give us continuity and keep us from having to start over again with each new generation. It will give us all—the young and the old—a power that will make our dreams come true.

Between God and Humanity

Some years ago we had a number of Vista workers here in the mountains of Eastern Kentucky. One, who was stationed in the county where I lived, came to talk to me several times, full of enthusiasm and new ideas. He told me that it wouldn't be long before all sorts of good things happened. The superintendent of schools was co-operating with his new ideas, the county judge was helping, and everything was working according to plan.

He said poverty and despair would soon be just a memory.

I was pleased to see this obviously dedicated young man so hard at work. I asked him if he had talked to God about his plans.

"What does God have to do with all this?" he asked me.

I told him it had been my experience that without God we cannot endure, especially in the face of the many deep problems of Appalachia.

"I don't believe in God," he told me. "I'm not out to destroy anyone else's beliefs, but I don't need God. And I don't think He's needed here.

We have the resources and the power and the abilities to do many good things without God."

I liked this young man, and for the sake of Appalachia, I truly hoped he could accomplish his plans. But I had to tell him what I really felt.

I said, "Without God, all your plans are doomed. You will not be here a year from now."

He laughed and said I was wrong and that he would prove it. "A year from now our programs will be running full steam and we'll be starting many new ones."

I watched him leave with sadness, because I felt that he had the talent and drive to do a great deal—if he would only offer it up to God. Without a bridge between himself and God he was destined to fail.

A few months later his conversations with me took a pessimistic turn. He couldn't understand why everything didn't go according to plan. He said people were going back on their word.

Finally, after about six months or so he began to talk about leaving. Less than nine months after our first conversation, he came to say good-bye.

I asked him if he remembered that conversation nine months earlier. He said he did.

"You were contacting everyone except God," I told him. "You had no roots to keep you strong when storms came along. Without the true strength that comes only from God, you cannot succeed."

I tell this story not because I was right and he was wrong, but because I believe that without God, without Jesus as a bridge between our lives and God, we cannot succeed in these mountains.

The advent of coal mining and the workings of governments since the time of the Civil War, including the programs of the Great Depression, and the New Frontier, have failed to solve our problems. We lag farther behind than ever.

We have forgotten to put God first. If my work has any value it will not be because of my brains or talent or drive or new ideas. It will be because, in a very simple and ordinary way, I welcome Christ, the greatest bridge builder of all time. He came to earth to build an everlasting bridge between God and man, between heaven and earth.

The bridge He built will last for eternity.

We must have the same philosophy, or we can accomplish nothing that will last.

Too often religious leaders become fiercely denominational. I, of course, belong to a denomination and love it deeply. I would lay down my life for the Catholic Church. But if we are not careful, denominations can be like roadblocks on the bridges we are trying to build.

Our religion should not be narrow. Religion needs, of all things, to be expansive. I don't mean nebulous or without strong values. I mean we should accept God completely and without hesitation. Faith is the only thing that will sustain us in these mountains.

In forty years of working in these mountains there have been many times when I have grown weary of it all. There are days when I've seen too many wretched houses with walls falling down and the wind coming through cracks in the walls. I've seen too many little children abused and ignored. I've seen too many lonely old people, too many illiterate adults, too much heartache and too much pain. Sometimes I just want to see joy. I want to hear songs and see people happy, well-fed and enjoying themselves.

Sometimes I want to get away from the mountains, where the lives of the people reflect the landscape with its deep valleys and sky-reaching peaks. I'd like to live on the plains where life is smooth and more secure.

A few days before the accident put me in this convalescent home, I was pulling out of my driveway when a man came running up. He beat on the window and asked me to stop. I was tired and had many things to do, and I'm sorry to say I just wished he would go away. Reluctantly, I rolled down the window to see what he wanted.

He said he needed help—the last thing I wanted to hear. His daughter was sick and they had made an appointment in Lexington, 125 miles away. She had to go for two days of tests and they had no money for the gasoline to get there. He asked me to lend him $35.

I was annoyed. I thought, "There must be 100,000 people this man could ask, all of whom have more money and more time than I have. Why is he bothering me?"

For five seconds I considered telling him to go elsewhere. Then he told me that he had already been everywhere he could think of and no one would help him. I was his last hope.

I gave him the $35.

I haven't seen him since my accident so I don't know if he will repay my $35. I'm not sure I care anymore whether he does or not, because after he left, I realized that I hadn't really lent the money to a poor man who desperately wanted to help his daughter.

I had lent the money to Christ Jesus.

That's who really came running up to knock on my car window that day. Jesus said that whenever we help the least of His brothers or sisters, we help Him.

Until we see Jesus in every human being with a need and until we strive to become like our Lord, we will never succeed in Appalachia. We won't have the vision to see the people's real needs, and we won't have the courage to continue when things go sour.

The victory in these mountains will not go to the rich or to the strong but to the one who will suffer and still endure.

The formation of the Christian Appalachian

Project, and the work it has done to improve people's lives, has never really been my work. It has been Jesus' work done through my hands and the hands of thousands of others. While I hold the title of Chairman of the Board at CAP, Jesus holds the title of Lord and Savior of us all. Only He has the power to use CAP as a bridge between God and humanity.

That's why, for forty years, I have tried to understand the dreams Jesus has for His people so I can try to see as He sees, listen as He listens and be enthusiastic as He is enthusiastic.

While there is time, we must continue this. We cannot grow tired. We must recognize Christ Jesus in every human being with a need. We must offer our hands, our hearts and our minds to help God's people in Appalachia.

Then we must have faith.

We cannot solve Appalachia's problems without faith. No matter how much money we have, we will be doomed to fail just as that Vista man did years ago. In the end, the people of Appalachia are God's people, not CAP's people.

The bridge that Jesus built between God and His people is our only real hope.

Over Troubled Waters

One day a young woman came to me and asked me to speak to her father-in-law. I knew the man slightly. He was a member of the city council in the town where I was living, was involved in coal mining and automobile racing and was fairly affluent. He was not the type I would have imagined would need our help, but she told me he had suffered large losses in the depressed coal industry. He had started drinking heavily, and was going through a painful divorce from his wife of 30-odd years. They were selling their home to settle the divorce. Then a young man who worked for him as a truck driver had a serious accident and wrecked a coal truck. Because of his financial problems, the man couldn't get the truck fixed. This was the proverbial straw that broke the camel's back. He sank into a terrible depression, holed himself up in the small apartment he was renting and started talking about killing people, including himself. His daughter-in-law desperately hoped I could help.

Because I feel strongly that it is my duty and the duty of the Christian Appalachian Project to be a bridge over troubled waters, I went to see him.

With some trepidation I walked up the stairs to his apartment and knocked on the door. He said to come in, so I opened the door slowly and entered the dim room.

The man was sitting on a chair next to a rifle propped against a couch. I said hello and introduced myself. He immediately told me that he had been out that day looking for the young man who had wrecked his truck. He was so angry he was going to shoot him. He said he didn't find him that day, but he would find him soon and kill him.

I told him that was no way to find peace; he had to find peace with God first. He began to curse and swear, and said he didn't want to know anything about God. "Where was God when I needed Him?" he asked.

He said he was so angry with God that he didn't want me to say His name in that house. He said he'd make me leave if I mentioned God again.

I said, "Well if that's the way you feel, you could go kill that young man or even kill yourself. But what purpose would that serve? All you'll do is leave your grandchildren with a horrible memory of you. Right now they love you and think you are special. You're their grandfather. You can ruin that love forever. Is that what you want to do? Do you want to do that much harm to your little grandchildren?"

The man began to cry.

He said, "I don't want to destroy their image of

me and make them ashamed of me forever. But there is no hope now."

I told him, "There is hope because you are still a child of God. You may not want to hear His name, but I'm telling you that He is here."

"He doesn't hear me. He doesn't love me," he sobbed.

"He hears you now more than ever," I said. "When you fail, when you stumble, when you sin the most, He loves you most dearly. He reaches out to take you home. Jesus said that He would always leave the 99 sheep to find the one that strayed."

Somehow the love of God was reaching this man because he got up and put the gun away—it had been cocked the entire time. I asked him to take the bullets out and he did. He told me I had given him new hope that God loved him. When I left him I felt he had a chance.

I have checked on him from time to time since then. He has not solved all his problems yet, but he hasn't killed anyone and he hasn't taken his own life. He is allowing God back into his life, and one of these days I know his troubled waters will pass.

So many times I have seen the calamities of life strike down the people of the mountains. When you live as close to the edge as they do, it doesn't take much to push you over. When you fight for your daily bread and enough wood to heat your house through a cold winter day, you have no reserves to fall back on when the vagaries of nature or the economy strike.

Last summer I heard about the Hoskins family. They had an electrical fire that destroyed the trailer they were living in. The fire swept through so fast that they got out with only the clothes on their backs.

Sterling Hoskins, the father of the family, has not worked in years because he is disabled from an injury he incurred in a truck accident. His wife, Leah, works as a nurse's aide, but doesn't make much money.

How can a family rebuild their lives when they've lost everything?

Tom, one of our volunteers, learned about the fire when twelve-year-old Sally didn't show up to go to our summer camp. When he couldn't get the family on the phone, he drove out to their home only to find a charred hulk where their trailer had been.

Thanks to Tom's concern and hard work, we did everything we could to help.

Tom and several other volunteers went out and helped them pick their garden crop of beans and corn. They canned the food at our volunteer house because Leah didn't have the space or the equipment in their temporary home—a small camper lent to them by a friend. We also brought them blankets, clothing, food and a heater for the camper.

When school started in August, Sally and her brother both had a difficult time. Sally had been a straight-A student but she began failing. The stress of four people living in the tiny camper, without privacy or a quiet place to study, was taking its toll.

We helped the family find a temporary home at a mobile home park in town. We found them a used refrigerator, a stove and some used furniture. This change made all the difference in the world, and Sally's grades bounced right back up.

Sterling decided to build a new house on the lot where their trailer had been. He used the small amount of money they received from fire insurance plus his life savings to put in a foundation and a well and septic system. Then the money ran out.

To add burden on top of burden, Sterling had to undergo surgery to correct hardening of the arteries in his legs.

He hopes to finish the house this spring when he is feeling better and can get some friends to help him. In order to save him money, CAP gave him windows and doors that had been donated to us.

We can't solve all the Hoskins' problems, and they still suffer a great deal and will continue to suffer the effects of their loss for many years. But we will continue to help the family in any way we can to get them back on their feet.

We try to be a bridge over troubled waters so

that people don't give up and don't lose hope. There will always be troubled waters. There will always be floods, fires, accidents, deaths, and lost jobs. But that isn't what life is about. Life is what you do with those things that happen to you. It's not the ingredients, but how you put them together that determines whether you find success, happiness and peace in life. The Scriptures say that virtue is made perfect in adversity. You can throw up your hands at adversity or you can grow.

CAP teaches growth.

When we write letters to people across the country to tell them that there is a place in America where great poverty and great troubles exist, it is not to gain their pity at our plight. We ask them to join us in overcoming these troubles, to help us build bridges and create something more beautiful than we ever had before.

Between the Hungry and the Well-Fed

I was a child of the Great Depression. I think that's why I understand and hate poverty so much. I especially hate the shame. I can still feel it, fifty years after the Great Depression ended.

One day, Mother and Father and I went to visit my brother in a Cincinnati hospital where he had undergone a hernia operation. In order to get to Cincinnati we had to cross a bridge that had a toll of ten cents, which in those days was a fair amount of money.

On the way home we got on the bridge but when we came to the toll booth my father sped up instead of slowing down. "We didn't pay the toll. We didn't pay the ten cents," I cried out.

"Quiet," my mother said, "We don't have ten cents."

I have never forgotten that feeling of helplessness and shame. When I see that same helplessness and shame in the poor of Appalachia, my heart breaks.

We who lived through the depression know about poverty—we all experienced it together. Those who didn't have a harder time understanding the trials the people of Appalachia are living every day.

I remember that we all helped each other as much as we could. When we visited my aunt's house she fed us and gave my parents meat and bacon. We got by with used clothing. The church gave us coal. A man in town let us purchase a cow on credit so that my brothers and sisters and I would have milk. Without that help I don't know how we would have survived.

There is a great myth in the American mystique that says that poor people should be able to pull themselves up by their bootstraps—that they should be self-sufficient.

Real life is not that simple.

My father worked three jobs. He worked for the WPA, he sold Watkins products door-to-door and on weekends he did carpentry. Still it was not enough—and many people in Appalachia face a similar treadmill. They can never catch up without help.

The Christian Appalachian Project exists to build bridges between the rich and the poor. When I talk to people at churches, in civic groups, on radio and TV, I am constantly told, "We didn't know there was poverty like this in America."

Our society has become stratified and segregated. We live in nice neighborhoods and don't cross to the other side of the tracks anymore.

Even our national infrastructure hides the poor.

In the past, the winding roads people traveled took them by the homes of poor people. Nowadays people zip by on the interstates at 65 miles an hour gazing at the lovely mountains. They never realize that three minutes off the next exit there are people who can't afford to heat their homes in the winter and children who go to bed hungry.

I think of three little boys CAP rescued. The boys, ages six, eight and eleven, lived with their father in a filthy old trailer in a hollow in one of our poorest counties. When a CAP volunteer first visited the family she was shocked.

The boys' mother had died three years earlier, and their father was a hopeless alcoholic. There was no food in the house. All the boys were thin and malnourished. The lack of food has stunted their growth. Eight-year-old Gary looks like a preschooler.

The children were dirty from head to toe. Their teeth were rotten because they hadn't seen a toothbrush in years.

When our volunteer explained the plight of these poor little boys, we went to work immediately. With great difficulty, we convinced their father to let us care for the boys for a while. Then we contacted the local authorities and urged them to take strong, prompt action on behalf of the children and arrange for counseling for their father. We knew that without rehabilitation, he was incapable of caring for his children.

The boys responded immediately to good food and lots of love. Three meals a day, soap, clean clothing and running water were new experiences for them.

Few people could hear of how poverty and neglect have tortured these three little boys, and not want to help. CAP bridges the gap between children like these and the well-meaning, generous people across America. We don't have the resources here in Kentucky to help all those who need help. We are only instruments working with the love of generous people everywhere.

Some of our donors are wealthy and live in fine homes in big cities and exclusive suburbs. They want to share their plenty and give something back to God's people. Many of our most loyal supporters, though, are middle-class Americans who believe that no one can be comfortable and happy when members of our human family are suffering in Appalachia. Many are hardly better off than those we serve. They give out of their own need in a great sacrifice of friendship.

All of them are building bridges between their lives and hearts and the people of the mountains.

When I go out to talk to our supporters I come back strengthened because of their eagerness to help the poor, their eagerness to be a part of a better tomorrow. America is still a beautiful place. Americans will still respond when they are aware. When we show them a great need and demonstrate

our ability to use the money wisely and judicious-
ly, they give with great generosity.

.Looking back on 40 years of building this bridge
between the poor and those better off, I see mountains of food, furniture and building supplies. I see
books and toys and fuel.

When I look a little deeper I see other things the
money has provided that can't be measured. I see
thousands and thousands of people better educat-
ed than they would have been. I see the smiles of
the elderly poor at the simple gift of fuel to heat a
drafty house, or food to fill a hungry belly. I see
the joy in the faces of children who are learning
and growing at our child development centers. I
see new strength that grows with each passing day.

I see hope.

A few weeks ago I was driving in a snowstorm
and slid off the road. I guess I haven't had much
luck driving lately. Anyway, I hit a tree and ruined
the car. It had 125,000 miles on it and was not
worth repairing. A day or so later a car salesman
called and said he heard I was looking for a used
car.

The salesman was a young black man in an area
where only one out of 365 or so people are black.
He grew up in a mining community where I often
preached in the streets. We opened a swimming
pool for children there, and a youth center and a
used clothing store. In spite of his family's poverty
he had experienced the love of Americans who

generously support our work. He said he had known poverty and loneliness and prejudice and he wanted to help repay CAP's kindnesses. He arranged to sell me an excellent used car worth a good deal more than he asked for it.

I know another man, who was once in need of food and help himself, who now helps others. He is one of the elderly citizens in our elderly visitation program. The volunteer who visited him thought he and his wife could benefit from a home garden so she worked with our garden seed program to get him seed potatoes, vegetable seeds, fertilizer and canning equipment. He planted a huge garden in his backyard and worked it all summer long.

When harvest time came he had a beautiful crop of potatoes, tomatoes, beans, carrots and more. He and his wife canned it all and found that there was far more than they could eat themselves.

He began distributing his food to needy neighbors and families that had been burned out of their homes. He took our little gift of seeds and turned it into his own fine act of sharing.

These stories are just a few examples of what happens when we build bridges between the rich and the poor, the hungry and the well-fed. Bridges go both ways and the people of Appalachia will give back to America even more than she shares with them.

Between Volunteers and the Poor

In December of 1950 we began to build a new bridge, in many ways the most important bridge we have ever built. It is a deeply personal bridge that has grown and grown between the people of Appalachia and the rest of the nation.

That Christmas of 1950 was the first time I asked people to volunteer their help in an organized way, to help build an outdoor nativity stable for the church in Berea. People responded generously, and I saw a great untapped resource that could change Appalachia forever—and change the lives of the volunteers who had talents they wanted to give back to God.

In the 40 years since that Christmas, 40,000 people have helped in one way or another. Some gave weekends, some weeks, some months and some years. Some came for a few weeks and have spent the rest of their lives here.

They have done beautiful things. They've repaired homes, visited the lonely and the sick, brought the light of truth to the young and the old, and helped children find themselves at our youth camps. They have shared letters and sometimes the

Bible with people who can't read. They have helped countless people plant gardens to fight the evil of malnutrition that plagues so many in Appalachia. They have taken the elderly to doctor's appointments and braved snow and cold to spread joy by distributing Christmas packages.

There is little that is noble and good that they have not done in God's name.

When our volunteers are through serving we try very hard to make sure they know how much we appreciate them. But time after time they tell me, "Father, we got much more than we gave!"

They found that when they stepped across the bridge of friendship, someone came over from the other side to befriend them. They found their own lives blessed because they acted a prayer of blessing.

I recently met a woman who volunteered with CAP 15 or 20 years ago as a high school student. I remember her because I asked her to cook meals for eight or nine other volunteers at one of our youth centers. She told me she had never cooked before, but she did very well and by the end of the six weeks she was cooking like an old hand. Before she left she begged me not to tell her mother she knew how to cook, because she had always gotten out of cooking at home by pleading ignorance.

She came back to help us again and again during her school years. At the time, we were helping people grow cucumbers because they were easily sold and had immediate cash value. She was a major force in this important farm program.

Today she works with a group in Cincinnati that reaches out to the people from Appalachia who move to the cities, without job skills or a decent education. She told me that some years ago she was engaged to a wonderful young man. When he proposed, she told him she had dedicated her life to helping the people of Appalachia and if he couldn't believe in her commitment and accept it, she couldn't marry him.

When she told me this I was both shocked and pleased. This was a woman of great commitment and faith. The few weeks she spent with us helped her find meaning and direction for her life that has inspired her ever since.

Her young man knew a good thing when he saw it and went ahead and married her. And today she is still building bridges between herself and the people of Appalachia.

I remember another young lady who volunteered one summer. She was a teacher in Ohio and was engaged to be married the following spring. She helped in our Bible school, visited the elderly and worked in our garden seed program. One day, just before she was due to return home, she was helping me clear some brush from a field. She told me she had a crisis. She wanted to know if she should marry the man she was engaged to.

I asked, "Do you love him?"

She said that she thought she did but she wasn't sure she could accept the kind of life she would have with him. The young man came from a well-to-do family. Their lives would be full of country clubs and social parties. They would live in a fine house in an exclusive neighborhood. She told me that after all she had seen in her time with us, she wasn't sure she could live that life.

I told her not to be too rash. I said that to be rich by itself was not evil. God needs and uses us all, and the world needs rich people too. I told her to pray and ask God's advice, not mine.

At Thanksgiving she wrote and told me she had broken off the engagement and wanted to come back as a permanent volunteer. Soon after she returned, she fell in love and married a young man who worked at CAP. They still live in the area and have started a business together that grosses one million dollars a year and employs 25 people in this area of terribly high unemployment.

She still doesn't live the high life, but she lives a good life. She and her husband live in Appalachia in a modest house. They reinvest the profits of the business to create more jobs.

Where but in America could this story take place? No one twisted her arm to make her give up the easy life. She gave up security and comfort because she wanted to be part of a solution. She has made a difference, her husband has made a difference, and I'm sure her children will make a difference.

She has built bridges.

One of my favorite CAP families has now grown to include three generations of volunteers. They originally began helping us in 1960 at CAP's camp on Herrington Lake in South Central Kentucky.

One New Year's Day Alan had a heart attack and died, leaving his wife, Rita, with five children, one only two years old. That summer she asked me if we could use a cook at our summer camp. I said we desperately needed a cook but that I didn't have any money to pay her. She said she'd work for food only, so we found a used trailer for her and her children and she cooked for our camp that summer.

Her children became a part of CAP too. Through the years they helped out in whatever way they could. One of the girls, Bonnie, volunteered the whole summer after she graduated from high school. Then after she got married, she came back often to visit her mother and helped in whatever CAP was doing.

Rita stayed with us ten years until one day she, too, had a heart attack and our Lord took her home.

After her mother's death, Bonnie followed her husband in his Naval career but kept in touch and I learned that they were blessed with three children. Everywhere she and her husband went, they volunteered and the children were taught by example to do the same.

A few months ago she sent me a newspaper clipping from the Orlando Sentinel. On the front page of the paper was her teen-age daughter, Katie. She was standing next to President Bush being given an award as an outstanding volunteer, number 36 of President Bush's One Thousand Points of Light.

I think of Katie—a third generation volunteer—and of Bonnie and Rita, and I wonder where this bridge will end. It all started with a woman willing to donate her time for God's work. I must admit some pride, too, at the distance CAP's bridges have spanned.

The other day someone reminded me of one of my favorite volunteers, Bill Eyle. I had been working in a town building a church, a children's camp and a store where we could distribute used clothing. A Lexington newspaper had run a small story about my dreams and Bill saw it.

He told me I was crazy. He said he knew how much prejudice there was against Catholics, and he couldn't imagine that I would come voluntarily where people would not appreciate my efforts.

Then he said his Pappy always told him, "Don't leave crazy people alone. Watch over them and be with them."

He said, "So if you don't mind, I'd like to come and help you."

"What can you do?" I asked.

He told me he was good at building, and I told him he was just the man I needed. He worked full time to help me build whatever project we had going. Whenever I needed him he was there.

One day we were building a camp in Jackson County. It was lunch time and as we were eating, I asked several college students who were helping, why they had volunteered. Some said that it was an adventure because they had never been away from home. Others said they wanted to discover Appalachia and help the poor. They all had good reasons. Then I asked Bill, who was seventy at the time, why he was there.

He told us that he had always wanted to volunteer and help others and do God's work, but he married young and had 10 children. He had to work hard to support them and make their lives secure, and before he knew it, his children had children of their own and his youth had slipped away. He had never been able to do what he really wanted to do. Then when he saw the newspaper article about this foolish priest, he knew his time had finally come.

When he finished speaking there was a deep silence. The young people looked at him. Here he was an old man who needed no excuse to just take it easy and retire and relax. Yet he had a dream to help and work for God. I think the young people were just as inspired as I was, listening to him tell his story.

I tell young people that no one can replace them in the work of God, that each person has a role to play. I think God was waiting for Bill all those years. He knew he would someday need Bill's special talents and abilities—no one else would do.

A young man recently presented this idea to me in a very powerful way.

He was a young priest of the Columban order from Nebraska. He was a wonderful volunteer and one of those rare people who always wears a smile and can find joy in the midst of great confusion and adversity. He had come to work with us summer after summer until one year he told me he wouldn't be back.

I asked him why, horrified that we might lose his talents and his energy and his love for God's people. He said he would be going to the Philippines to work with the poor there. I asked whether he had given up his plan to be a college professor at a Catholic university. He told me education was still important to him, but he thought others could replace him in the ranks of college professors.

He said, "I'm not sure others will replace me in the Philippines."

That statement sums up volunteering. There is work to be done here that can only be done by some of the individuals who will read this book. I don't know who you are, only you and God know.

Some of you are youngsters looking for a mission and a calling. Some are adults with the freedom to give a weekend or a month or a summer or even a year. Some are seniors who have retired and have time and skills and wisdom no one else can duplicate. All of you have a calling to build bridges.

If you come here you won't make a lot of money. We'll give you a place to live, good food, and a few dollars spending money.

The work is not easy. There are times when the poverty is depressing. There are times when you'll want to take the afternoon off rather than go and be with an elderly woman who has no other contact with the outside world. There are times when you'll be rebuffed by families that resist even the kindest gesture. There are times when you think you'll scream if you see another child being raised in squalor.

But it is wonderful work, because there are more times when you'll find that your helping hand means the difference between hope and despair—when your words convince a mother to send a child to school, when your own hands build a new home for a family who has lost theirs, when you see the edges of poverty move back a small step and the people rejoice.

It is the work of building bridges—God's work. There is no better.

To the World of Education

Little Ricky has learned a lot in his five short years of life. He knows how to drink alcohol, smoke cigarettes, and cuss and swear with the best of them.

Unfortunately, those are not the things he needs to learn to build a future.

One of our workers met Ricky and his mother a few years ago and made it her goal to get Ricky into one of our child development centers and help him prepare for school.

It has been a struggle. Ricky's mother is illiterate. His father abandoned her and her four children. They live in a run-down trailer. She cooks on a wood stove and lives from day to day with no plan, no future.

She wants desperately to hold on to her children because they are all she has to live for. She doesn't understand the value of education. She knows so little of any life other than that of her own parents, she sees little need to send her children to school. She has kept them home until the school system demands that she send them at age seven.

By that age, her older children were hopelessly

behind their peers. All three have learning disabilities and will need special education throughout their school years. Our worker is determined that Ricky, the baby of the family, not suffer the same fate.

She visited the little boy and his mother often and become great friends with Ricky. She told them all about one of our child development centers—that there were toys, and other kids Ricky's age, and that he would have lots of fun. She told them that Ricky would have a nutritious lunch and that he would learn how school worked so that when the time came for him to go to public school he would be ready.

Ricky's mother remained unconvinced.

It was Ricky who finally won the day. He begged his mother to let him go to school. She couldn't hold out against that kind of pressure so she finally agreed to let him go.

Last September Ricky started attending a CAP child development center. Our van picks him up in the morning and he's always bright and cheerful. He loves school. He has adjusted to the teachers and the other students, and he has become one of the best block tower builders in the whole class.

His mother is learning too. To give mothers an opportunity to take responsibility for their children's educations, and to stretch our funding dollars, each mother works at the child development center two days each month. Ricky's mother helps make meals and has learned a lot about good nutrition and health. She has seen good parenting role models.

So, the education of Ricky and his mother has begun. They have started a journey that will never end. I pray that someday Ricky's mother will enroll in our literacy program and maybe even gain her high school equivalency diploma. We'll be there to help, every step of the way.

Whenever we discuss the problems of the Appalachian people, the need for education always comes up first. Isolated for 200 years, reliant on coal mining (an occupation that until recently required strong backs but not much school learning), many of the people of Appalachia have never learned the value of education. But these are not stupid people. In fact, I believe they hold a special intelligence born of the necessity for ingenuity to survive the harsh lives they lead.

One of my greatest dreams is that we will someday relight the fire of learning in Appalachia.

I hate to see grown men and women who can't count to ten, or read well enough to even do their grocery shopping. I see so many young people who go through school without learning anything of life-long use. I see old people whose lives are caged by illiteracy. They never experience the excitement that comes from reading of new ideas, new places and new dreams.

I mourn that so many people are cut off from

the Word of God because they can't read the Bible.

We have a long way to go. We have started six child development centers. We have a school, The Mountain Christian Academy, that includes grades one through eight. We offer scholarships to high school students who want to go on to college.

We need to do much more.

One of our most rewarding successes has been our adult literacy and GED programs. Throughout much of Eastern Kentucky, less than 50 percent of adults have high school diplomas. For many of the mountain people, education is not a high priority. They are more concerned with finding a job to feed themselves and their families. They often realize too late that they have traded freedom for a short-term job. They will be forever trapped and limited by their ignorance.

Our GED program encourages adults who can read and write to earn a high school equivalency certificate. We hold classes to go over the material, and we help them arrange to take the state GED tests. In three years we have helped more than 400 people get their diplomas. This may not seem like a large number at first, but it is an excellent start. As those people tell others of the benefits of this education: better jobs, more advancement, an increase in the quality of life, the number of people who want to return to their education is rising dramatically.

Our School on Wheels program trains volunteer tutors who drive to isolated homes to teach adults to read and write or help them study for the GED test. Some of those who have been taught have been so grateful for this new-found treasure that they have volunteered to teach others.

In this way we rekindle the fires of learning, building a bridge to the world of knowledge. Jesus said the truth would set us free. We are building a bridge that allows people to find that truth.

Education does not only mean learning to read and write. It can also mean learning to master yourself and overcome fears. Sometimes it means learning how to dream. At our summer camps we take children who have been isolated in the hollows of Appalachia and show them that there is a big world outside, a world filled with all kinds of people and all kinds of things to do.

I remember a young boy who had witnessed his brother's drowning in the creek near his home. When he came to our camp last summer, he was terrified of the water and refused to go in. Little by little our camp counselors coaxed him into the water. At first, he shook with fear, but by the end of his stay he could swim with a life preserver. Now he wants to learn to swim unassisted.

By helping him overcome his fear, we taught him an important lesson that will carry him through hard times all his life.

Many years ago I met a boy named Lester, who

came from a very poor family. His mother enrolled him in the grade school at the Catholic Church in Lancaster because his sisters were failing in the public schools. Although he was not a great student, Lester did well enough to graduate from the eighth grade just before we closed the school for lack of money. Unfortunately we lost track of Lester after that. I later heard that he dropped out during his freshman year in high school.

One day Lester showed up at CAP, looking for a job. He said he would do anything for work. I told him we had a small press that we used to print newsletters, and that we had a job for him there if he wanted it.

Things went very well for a while. Lester was excited to be learning a new trade.

Then the supervisor started to notice that things were missing around the print shop. He suspected Lester was stealing them and asked me to speak to Lester.

I asked Lester if he were stealing from CAP. At first I could see in his face that he wanted to lie and deny that he had taken anything, but he broke down and told me the truth.

I told him that we valued honesty, and that trust was very important. I gave him one more chance and told him that if he had problems he should come and talk to me. For a while he did well. Then we began to miss things again.

I told Lester that it was obvious that he was not

yet serious about his life and I could not help him until he was.

Then I fired him.

We parted on friendly terms and I convinced him that if he ever became committed to improvement we would be here to help.

Several years later I bumped into Lester again. I was driving to a CAP meeting in Lancaster and I was a bit early, so when I noticed a business I hadn't seen before, I decided to stop in. I must admit it was not just any business, it was a boat dealership. I have always had a great weakness for boats, and I had to stop and see what this new business was all about.

A young man came over and asked if I needed any help. I said I was wondering how long the business had been there and how it was going. He said they had only been open a few months, but it was going pretty well.

Then he looked at me and said, "You don't remember me, do you, Father?"

He looked familiar, but I didn't remember his name. He said, "I'm Lester. I went to your school and you gave me a job . . . and you fired me."

I told him I did remember him and that I was glad to see him. I said I was sad when I lost track of him.

"I have wanted to tell you that I have never forgotten those things you taught me," he said. "You told me that no one gets a free ride. You told me that I couldn't take advantage of people and be a success. You said I had to be a part of the solution in my own life rather than part of the problem. I finally realized you were right, and I decided to change my life. I worked in construction for several years. When I had saved some money my partner and I started this business and we have done pretty well so far."

"I really and truly don't know how to thank you."

We talked for a while longer, and when I left I felt renewed. We had truly made a difference in one man's life. Later, at Christmas, I received a card from Lester. I will never forget it. Inside, under the usual wishes of Merry Christmas it said simply:

"Thank you for my life—Lester."

Lester's wife has now begun working for CAP. She's a wonderful young woman, and she, too, thanked me for all CAP had done to bring the best out in Lester.

And so, what looked like a lost cause had a happy ending because we taught one mixed-up young man the things that are important in life.

Sometimes people just need to learn marketable and useful job skills. I remember a man who wanted a job very badly. We had started a small woodworking shop in Jackson County making small gift items: bookends, candlesticks and things like that. I wasn't sure we could afford to put on any extra people, but I felt so strongly about this man's commitment that I decided to go ahead.

Three weeks later I got back up to visit the shop. The man pulled me aside and showed me his work. He told me he had never dreamed he could make things that were so beautiful and useful. He was filled with a new sense of pride and excitement about himself and what he could become.

That's what education is all about. It's not an end. It's a beginning. We are building the bridges and now, one by one, the people of Appalachia are stepping onto those bridges and bravely crossing over to a new world . . . a better world.

Between the National Economy and Appalachia

One day a little boy taught me a tragic lesson about Appalachia.

I was driving on a hot summer day and stopped at a general store for a soft drink. As I stood drinking the soda, I noticed a young boy sitting on the porch of a house across the road.

I went over and said hello and sat beside him on the porch. We talked for a while, and I asked him what he wanted to be when he grew up.

"I reckon I'd like to be like my Pap," he said with great pride.

Well, that was fine. Most young boys want to be like their dads, if, of course, they don't want to be a fireman or a policeman. I asked him what his father did.

He said simply, "He rocks."

I assumed he meant a mason or a stoneworker, both age-old trades of great value. I asked him, "What kind of rocks does he work with?"

The little boy looked at me strangely and said, "He doesn't work with rocks. He rocks in his chair on the porch."

When I left the boy there was a great load on my

heart. I thought, "Is this how far welfare has come?"

It has made an idle man out of this boy's father and so ingrained that life on this family, that the boy believes that's what people do—rock on the porch, watch the cars go by and wait for the first of the month when the welfare check comes.

I am not opposed to welfare. Welfare is charity and we have to be a people to whom charity is deeply important. If we are not charitable we cannot call ourselves people of God.

But there has to be more. When we have resources to share with others, we are obligated to share in the wisest and most constructive way possible. We have to understand what the people really need and how solutions can come about.

Today we have a tragic distortion of our need to be charitable. We feel we must give money to the needy to assuage our guilt. But money will not cure poverty because it cannot change people's hearts. Too often our welfare system is a system of enslavement.

When people try to get off welfare they find that there are no jobs, or at best, minimum wage jobs. To take such a job, they must give up the security and health benefits of welfare. There's little wonder that we have families in Appalachia who have been on welfare for three generations.

That is a sin.

There can be solutions though. We need to

build bridges between the economy of Appalachia and that of the rest of the country. The people of Appalachia are not shiftless. Life here is often hard and the mountain people work hard simply to survive. They work with great diligence and effort when they know there is a just reward.

Repairing the economy of Appalachia is not a hopeless dream. Appalachia is rich in natural resources. We have one of the most abundant supplies of energy in the world. The coal buried under these mountains will last for many decades if we can mine and use it without damaging our environment. There are also great deposits of oil and natural gas.

We possess great hardwood forests. We have limestone and sand for building.

From the late 1800s to the present, people with money and vision have come to Appalachia to develop these resources. But too often, the money made by extracting these resources went out of the region. Little has been reinvested here. Although vast fortunes have been made from Appalachian coal and timber, we still have the lowest standard of living of any region of America.

In the last 100 years, coal has been in a boom-and-bust cycle. Today it is in a downturn, and until we find better ways of using coal it will probably remain so. Today's coal mines are so heavily mechanized that fewer and fewer miners are needed to extract the coal. That may be a blessing in disguise, because throughout history, coal mining has rarely paid wages commensurate with the risks from injury and black lung disease.

If only the money being made from coal could be reinvested into building new profitable industries here.

Not only have we stopped growing here in Appalachia, we are often going backwards. Many jobs have been lost as labor-intensive industries move their operations to Third World countries where wages are dramatically lower.

The rest of the country has lost much of its ability to absorb Appalachian young people. The industrial centers of Cincinnati, Indianapolis, Detroit and Chicago have their own problems.

With all these factors it would seem impossible to revive the economy of Appalachia. But I know that's not the case.

Step by step, business by business we can succeed. We need a great deal of creativity. The solutions will not be obvious. We won't be able to simply duplicate the Silicon Valley here in Eastern Kentucky.

But there are other things we can do. For example, last year we created a special program to teach entrepreneurial skills to people without jobs. We screened dozens of people and chose 13 who had the desire and the drive to start a business.

We taught them business management skills, and we helped them put together business plans and get financing. We asked local business people to speak to our budding entrepreneurs so they could learn from those who are already successful. Out of that group of 13 people, four started businesses, and two went back to school to get the training they needed to make their business ideas work.

One of the entrepreneurs started a rabbit farm. Rabbit farming is not an obvious solution to the problems of Appalachia, but it is a creative and workable one. Rabbit meat is low in fat and cholesterol, important considerations in today's health-conscious society. Rabbits grow rapidly and are one of the most efficient domesticated animals for converting grain to protein. Unlike most other livestock farming, you don't need lots of flat land—a commodity in short supply in Appalachia. And everyone knows how fast rabbits multiply.

Who knows, maybe Appalachia will become the rabbit capital of the nation!

Another one of our entrepreneurs really does work with rocks. He started a masonry business that employs six people in a county with one of the highest unemployment rates in Kentucky.

A little rabbit farm and a small masonry business won't recreate a vibrant economy here, but this program has become a bridge that has helped a few creative, energetic Appalachian people find solutions. We need more programs like this.

CAP has helped start dairy farms, saw mills, greenhouses, furniture building and repair businesses, and more. Sometimes we provided the seed money, sometimes the technical assistance and contacts with local banks and professional people. Always we built bridges.

I have a pet project—to start a stained glass industry in Appalachia. Producing stained glass is a labor-intensive craft that fits the artistic soul of the Appalachian people. There is a great market for stained glass for churches, funeral homes, restaurants, private homes and businesses. Its lasting beauty has come back into vogue, and there is a shortage of manufacturers.

If we could find financial backers and entrepreneurs, I believe we have the artists and craftsmen to make Appalachia world famous for stained glass—and the people of Appalachia would gain a great sense of pride and accomplishment at creating something of lasting value.

Private enterprise motivated by Christian ethics and a sense of public responsibility is a most powerful force for good. I hope our friends across the country who are entrepreneurs or who have money they want to invest, will open their minds to see that Appalachia can be profitable, and open their hearts to join in this noble cause. Investing in Appalachia can be a replacement for simple charity. I believe its effects will be longer lasting—and it will help us break the chains of welfare dependency that imprison the people.

There are more than enough resources in America to heal our troubles. There are more than enough creative people to put an end to the apathy and despair. We need a bridge that connects Appalachia to the big companies, little companies and individual investors that make America's economy run. Until we build that bridge, and build an economic base separate from coal, we will be fighting against the current.

If we create that bridge, the natural resourcefulness, determination and drive of the mountain people will take over, and little boys and girls will no longer want to grow up to rock on the porch.

Between CAP and Other Organizations

In the sixties everyone was interested in Appalachia. Presidents Kennedy and Johnson took a personal interest and inspired the nation to care. Many churches set up organizations to help. Vista came, the Jesuits had a group here, and federal money was everywhere.

Many good things were done. Roads and schools were built. Water and sewer projects were completed.

Then came the seventies.

The New Frontier had come and gone, and budgets were tighter. We were paying for Vietnam and the oil embargo, and the economy was hurting. The federal money dried up.

The infighting began. I was saddened to see so many worthwhile organizations competing with each other. Because they were fighting for a shrinking pie, there were accusations made, and animosity and hard feelings developed. Everyone said, "Our group should get the money because we are doing the most good!"

This bickering was a tragic mistake. It distracted organizations from their good work and destroyed the cooperation that is the only hope for Appalachia. It broke down the bridges.

To this day I am proud that CAP never got involved in this battling. I decided early on that we would never depend on government money. I wanted to raise money by directly appealing to the generosity of America's people. I felt we had to sell our value to every man, woman, and child.

We wrote letters and newsletters telling people about the problems and what we were doing. We showed them our dreams.

Many people thought I was crazy. They said we were foolish to ignore the federal gold mine. But I stood my ground and said that a day would come when the federal money would end and that CAP was in this for the long haul.

When the fighting began, we stayed above it and tried to light a candle instead of curse the darkness.

Twenty years after the sixties ended, most of those organizations are gone, while CAP is still going and growing.

Those organizations had great value, and I don't believe CAP has all the answers or that CAP can accomplish everything in Appalachia. I wish we had those people back here by our sides with their sleeves rolled up ready to work.

I am determined to help those organizations that remain as well as the excellent new organizations. That's why I suggested to CAP's board of directors ten years ago that we give a percentage of our income to other worthwhile organizations working in Appalachia, no matter how noble our own programs and no matter how much we need the money. The board agreed and we have been doing this ever since.

Once again people tell me we are crazy. They point out that we always face terrible budget problems and debt ourselves. "How can you afford to give money away?" they ask.

But I never asked CAP to be a logical organization, only a Godly organization. The Bible tells us we must give not only from our excess but from our own need. Jesus singled out the widow who donated her last penny as the true believer, not the rich man who gave many times more but never felt any pain in doing it. He said to imitate the widow.

Over the years CAP's grants and loans have done great things for many people. We have helped fund day care centers, food pantries, housing projects, emergency assistance programs and many other worthwhile projects. In doing so we have helped bring out the best in people. Earlier I told the story about the minister from Topmost whose congregation decided to start giving to the poor every Christmas, inspired to be more of what God was calling them to—all because we gave them some used furniture.

This bridge between organizations in Appalachia, like all the other bridges we are building, goes in both directions. I am heartened by the response I get when I talk to businesses about donating to CAP. They donate building materials, books, medicines, food, and more. They see our work, and they want to walk across the bridge and help.

I have described the closemindedness that often permeates religion here in Appalachia, but that closemindedness doesn't have to be permanent. It can be erased if we build bridges between all the churches doing work for the poor.

A few years ago we set up an organization called SOAR, Spirit of the Appalachian Region. We committed ourselves to give $50,000 every year to worthy religious organizations.

At Christmas each year we give baskets of food, clothing and toys to needy families so they can share in the joy we celebrate on that holy day. Because we can't reach every needy family in every county, we invite pastors and others from churches all over Eastern Kentucky to pick up baskets to take to the needy in their communities.

I always get a special feeling when I see the pickup trucks and station wagons lined up. I meet ministers of every faith. Many tell me they have never met a Catholic priest before. Together we are building bridges that join our churches and help the people. A few years ago, in Magoffin County, we tried to hold a service in the center of a town but the pastor there wouldn't let us use his church.

He was afraid the poor would sully it. So we went outside the town and used a small church there. The minister was very accommodating and even took part in the service. After an hour or so of singing, praying and reflection, we started to go next door, where we had some refreshments.

Before I made it next door a man came up to me. He said he was a Baptist preacher and that he had long been a great and vocal critic of the Catholic Church. He admitted that he was so moved by our expression of solidarity and our generosity in helping the community that he was ashamed that he could ever have spoken against someone working in Jesus' name.

Then he startled me, and everyone else who was there. He told me that he had cancer and asked me to bless him that God might heal his body.

Tears rolling down my cheeks, I asked God with all my heart, to bless that man. I made the sign of the cross and invoked the name of Jesus, begging Him to use His healing power to heal this faithful brother of His. When I had finished, the crowd of people cheered and clapped.

It was a beautiful thing, an unthinkable thing that happened that day. It was a bridge built in one wonderful moment of sheer honesty.

The other day, when I was still in the hospital, I got a card from a lady who started God's Pantry, a food bank in Lexington, Kentucky. She collects food from businesses and manufacturers and gives it to people in need. Two years ago they were looking to expand to places in the mountains. We told them they could use our warehouse and we even supplied people to manage the operation.

The woman sent me the card to say that she hoped I was feeling better and that she hoped my accident wouldn't stop the work we were doing together. She didn't want the bridge between us to come down.

She needn't have worried, because as long as I have breath in my body—and hopefully even after I am gone—CAP will continue to build bridges and share our resources with other worthy organizations in Appalachia.

It may not be "good business." If it were, everyone would be doing it. Sometimes it doesn't make sense for us to give away what we could use ourselves. But that is exactly what the people who send money to support CAP do. How can we do any less than what we ask of them?

Jesus said that we should be like the Good Samaritan who gave freely and without regard to repayment, even though he was considered an enemy. The Good Samaritan was not interested in competition or the differences between people or organizations, he was interested in building bridges.

Jesus also said that when we give as the Good Samaritan did we will be repaid a hundredfold on earth and in the everlasting life in the world to come.

Our Lord's words have come true for CAP. The interest in Appalachia waned after those heady days of the sixties, but we are still here, still doing God's work and still building bridges.

How to Build a Bridge

Over the years of CAP's work in these lovely but troubled mountains, I have learned a foolproof formula for building bridges to help the people of Appalachia.

First we must understand the problem.

I don't mean from a scholarly point of view. I'm not talking about the 200-page, two-million-dollar studies done in Washington. I mean we need to talk to real people, meet with them and learn what is in their hearts. We need to live their problems with them day to day.

Second, we must design a solution with God's help. This means that we must look at the long-term. Band-aids and temporary fixes are not acceptable. We must use our precious resources of money and talent and energy to erase poverty, not cover it up. We need to build bridges that last.

Finally, and most important, we must ask ourselves why we are trying to solve this particular problem, and why we have chosen this particular solution.

If we are doing it for our own accomplishment, as something to add to our resumes, or to bring fame, we are destined to fail. Any work we do must be in God's name. It must be work that God would do.

If we can successfully meet these three conditions then I say, "Let's go to it!"

Often we don't have all the means. Usually we are praying for a long shot. But if we just start and if we work in God's name, He will be by our side. He will find the resources for us. He will call the people we need. We will never struggle alone.

This simple faith is the bedrock on which every one of our bridges is built.

Our faith should not be just of a certain dogma, but a total conviction that Jesus is "the way, the truth and the life." There is no other way but His way. The greatest obstacles to this kind of faith are reason, rationalization and attempts to predict the future.

I am not an advocate of irrationality but of spirituality—a rising above the ordinary and the reasonable. We must be convinced we follow Someone all wise, all powerful and all loving. If we truly believe, we never need fear.

If faith is the bedrock of our bridges, perseverance is the span.

Our Lord said to His apostles, "Not everyone who says to me, 'Lord, Lord', will enter the kingdom of heaven. Only one who does the will of My Father, will enter the Kingdom of Heaven."

The will of His Father is not for a day or a week

or a year. We can't bargain with God. We can't say, "Oh, I'll give God five years or ten years and then I'll go my own way."

That will never work. We have to be committed. You can never turn back from your calling nor take your hand off the plow.

Jesus said, "Follow me."

He didn't say for just a few years or a month or two. He simply said, "Follow me."

One of the enemies of perseverance is despair. It is easy to despair in Appalachia. The problems are so old and the people so ingrained in poverty that, at times, it seems the end will never come. Sometimes it makes me want to give up and go sit by a lake to rest. Sometimes it seems like every day— every hour—brings a new crisis.

But if we believe Jesus is by our side with every step, we can continue on. He won't let us fall and He won't abandon us. He said, "I am with you all days even until the end of time."

In the Sea of Galilee when the waves were crashing over the sides of the boat, the Apostles feared for their lives. Despair gripped them and they were afraid they would drown. They woke Jesus and said, "What are we going to do?"

I can imagine their faces. Some days I feel that same kind of fear. I don't fear for my life, but for the failing of my life's work. I want to ask God, "What are we going to do?"

But Jesus scolded his disciples when they woke

him. He said, "Ye of little faith. Why were you afraid? Did you not know that I am with you?"

When He spoke the sea grew calm and their fears were relieved. Whenever I feel the urge to panic and give up in despair, I remember Jesus' words. Then I take a deep breath and try to keep putting one foot in front of the other, trusting that if I stumble Jesus will catch me.

When we have that faith and that strategy of perseverance it should give us the confidence to be patient.

Patience is a virtue that has always come hard to me. When I was a younger man I wanted solutions now. I wanted to change people's lives today, or at least this week. I wanted to make lists of accomplishments.

But we have to be patient. The Kingdom of God will not come about overnight. Success is not ours to demand. In fact, God never promised us success at all. He promised He would be with us and that we should follow Him and be faithful to Him. That is enough.

The problems of Appalachia were created over the course of more than 200 years. Generations of Appalachian people have grown up in poverty and illiteracy. It may take generations to reverse this sad legacy. If we do not have patience we have already failed.

Many people who have come to visit me since my accident have asked me if I will retire now. By all logical rights I probably should. I don't yet know how mobile I will be when I have healed. I'm 66 years old. Even before this accident I had problems with my back. I am losing my vision in my left eye, and I have many of the normal impairments that come with age.

But then someone else will say, "Please don't quit. Who will take care of us? We can't lose you!"

I know I must persevere and have faith and patience. Whatever I have I must give. There is always a new frontier, a new mountain to climb, a new bridge to build. I am still excited about the work we are doing. I am still deeply in love with Appalachia and her people. I am still deeply in love with my church and my God.

In fact, with approaching age and with my accident as an exclamation point in my life, I grow ever more determined and eager. There is so much I want to accomplish.

Every morning when I wake up I hear God whispering in my ear, "Hey Beiting, get up and get going. My people need help."

So, I try to run even faster and even harder these days. I will never be able to sit on the porch in a rocking chair and watch the world go by. Not as long as a single member of God's family suffers in Appalachia.

How could I do otherwise? We all know the love of family. When a brother or sister is in need, your world stops and you do whatever you can to help. That is one of our most noble inspirations.

Jesus said that we are all brothers and sisters in God's family. Every little boy who can't read is our brother. Every woman who is trying to raise a family on her own is a sister in need. Every elderly woman who sits by herself in isolation and despair is our dear mother.

More and more these days, I see CAP's work as the work of a family. Like most families, not everyone has the same strengths or the same weaknesses. Some members are called to volunteer their time and their lives here in the mountains. Others are needed to provide the financial support that keeps CAP alive. Still others will be, for the time being, primarily receivers of help.

And many members of our family who were once in desperate need themselves, now have the strength and resources to help others.

Our CAP family extends to the far reaches of this great nation. Every member is critical. Every member is a worthwhile child of God. Every member is a key part of the bridge.

Earlier I said that I had a foolproof method of building bridges in Appalachia. I didn't mean that all our programs will work. I didn't mean that the solutions we are applying today are the ones that will succeed.

But if we follow these guidelines, we cannot help but build bridges. Bridges are not solutions.

They are paths to the future.

The future in Appalachia will be bright. I know this in my heart and I believe it in faith.

Someday the children will grow strong and healthy. Someday they will get good educations and there will be good jobs for all. Someday the people of Appalachia will live in good houses. Someday the elderly will once again be sources of wisdom and knowledge instead of lonely outcasts.

Someday we—you and I and the people of Appalachia—will walk across the bridges we have built into a new and better life.

EPILOGUE—Hubert Martin

Twenty years ago Father Beiting took me to see what he called Camp Andrew Jackson.

As we drove to the camp he described it to me. He said it had a lake and cabins and a baseball diamond, and more. He told me that poor children would have Bible School there, and do crafts and learn to swim.

When we finally got to the spot where he said the camp was, I saw nothing but fields full of weeds and wildflowers.

"Where's the lake?" I asked him.

Father Beiting said it was there. He showed me where the lake was, and where the cabins were. All I saw was grass and bushes but he walked me around the land describing Camp Andrew Jackson as if it were plain as day.

That day I learned what vision is. If anyone has ever had a vision of what life can be like in Appalachia it is Father Beiting.

I first met Father Beiting when my mother enrolled me in his new grade school in Lancaster, Kentucky. My sisters had been going to public school and not doing very well.

My grandmother and my mother knew Father Beiting and trusted him. Even though most people were leery of Catholics and the new school was to be run by nuns, my mother felt that if Father Beiting was involved, the school had to be something special.

We saw Father Beiting only occasionally at the school. Even in those days, back in 1955, he was driving more than a hundred thousand miles a year, serving the people of Appalachia and trying to raise support for the Christian Appalachian Project.

When we did see Father Beiting we tried desperately to be on our best behavior. Father Beiting is a big man, and to seven-year-olds he cut quite an imposing figure.

The worst thing anyone wanted to hear was Father Beiting saying, "Come over here, I want to talk to you."

I also remember that even when the public schools had days off because of snow, we had to go to school. Father Beiting's intense belief in education was not dimmed by a little snow.

I wish I could say that I was a star pupil in that school, but I wasn't. I did manage to complete all eight grades, though. And the day I graduated is one of my proudest memories of childhood.

Later, when I found out how hard it was to find a good job, I sought out Father Beiting's help. As always, he came through.

He gave me a job working in CAP's printing shop. I learned the printing business from the bottom up. Eventually I could run the printing press and the darkroom and most of the operation.

On another occasion I got into some trouble with the law. Father Beiting spent six hours in court with me, trying to convince the judge that I was basically a good kid. In the end I received a fine of $500 and three years probation. Father Beiting made sure I paid that fine and served my probation correctly. He told me that he still believed in me.

Somehow when Father Beiting believes in you good things happen in your life.

I didn't see Father for quite a while after that, but his words and his vision for my life stayed with me. I settled down and got married, and worked very hard in a construction business.

One day when I was on a construction job I heard loud music coming from down the street and I thought some kids had a boom box radio going. I walked down to see what was happening and there was Father Beiting, standing on a small platform preaching his heart out to a small crowd of people. I didn't disturb him and I returned to my work, but just watching him inspired me again to put my life in order and justify his faith in me. I hope I have done that. I now work in a small boat business. I'm trained as a boat mechanic, a carpenter and a printer. I do honest work and I support my family.

I try to help CAP whenever I can.

When I worked at the print shop I used to help Father Beiting deliver Christmas baskets to the poorest families in Appalachia. My own family was poor, but even I could not believe the poverty I saw on those trips with Father Beiting.

There were families living in shacks. The snow would blow right through the cracks in the walls and pile up on the floor. I was always amazed at the strength of the people and the great suffering they endured.

Even more so, I was amazed at Father Beiting's incredible energy and desire to help. I remember a time when he braved an angry man who threatened to shoot him, just so he could deliver a Christmas basket to the man's wife and children. Any other man I know would have given up and gone away.

Father Beiting's own determination and willingness to work carries over into everything CAP does. I remember how hard he worked CAP's volunteers. He certainly made them earn that one dollar a day that he paid them. I was always afraid he would drive them away, but they stayed.

One time he told me I could take a vacation. He suggested I go to New York City and see the sights and have a good time. When I got to New York I unpacked the trunk of the car and found a box full of slides and tapes about CAP. I also found instructions and a list of schools where I had appointments to show the slides and talk about Appalachia. I spent my "vacation" talking to high school students about the Christian Appalachian Project.

There's no doubt about it, Father Beiting can drive you crazy. He can also make you very proud of yourself, your life, and your faith in God.

Everything I now have I owe to him, and I am committed to helping him in whatever way I can.

Sometimes I feel great sadness for Father Beiting because I know he gets frustrated and he wants to help a great many more people than he has been able to so far.

Then I remember that day when he showed me Camp Andrew Jackson. Today the camp is real, with a man-made lake and cabins and joyful children—just the way he said it would be.

I know now that when Father Beiting has a vision of better things—even if to my eyes it still looks like a barren field—it's only a matter of time before his vision comes true.

The Mountain Spirit, Christian Appalachian Project's bimonthly magazine, will tell you about many of CAP's programs as we continue to work to help the poor of eastern Kentucky. It contains lots of poignant stories about the people of Appalachia—people like those mentioned in the book.

If you would like to subscribe to *The Mountain Spirit* (or renew your current subscription), please complete the order form below.

—————————————————————————

Subscription Order Form for *The Mountain Spirit*

Please enter my one-year subscription to *The Mountain Spirit*. Enclosed is my check for $5.00, made payable to CAP.

Name _____

Address _____

City _____ State _____ Zip _____

Kindly return this order form and your check to: Christian Appalachian Project, 322 Crab Orchard Road, Lancaster, KY 40446.

If You'd Like to
Learn More About the
Work of the Christian Appalachian Project . . .

. . . or if you would like additional copies
of this book, please write or phone us at
our headquarters:

Christian Appalachian Project
322 Crab Orchard Road
Lancaster, Kentucky 40446
(606) 792-3051

We deeply appreciate your interest and support!!